EFFECTIVE TECHNIQUES FOR DEPRESSION OVERCOMING

Empowering Strategies for a Brighter Tomorrow

Stephen N. Arnold

2

Contents

Copyright © 2023 by [M. Asif Nazir]

A Look at Anxiety

In this vast territory of human emotions, one frequently stumbles upon the rolling grounds of psychological landscapes. Of all these topographies, anxiety is the most peculiar in its landform. It has steep precipices, representing intense anxiety, and deep canyons for prolonged worries. Some of these landscapes are filled with anxiety that is puzzling to many. Consequently, academics and society should not only recognize these terrains but also comprehend their inner workings as guideposts on which they could navigate through their future. This is relevant to both scholarly and general audiences. Initially, in understanding worry, familiarity with a variety of its manifestations is key. Some individuals had claimed temporary aches comparable to whiffs of wind that flit across the otherwise serene pasture. This includes temporary instances, often called situational anxiety, that happen under specific pressures, like when approaching or about to face social gatherings. On the other hand, some individuals perceive their anxious lives as a continuing storm where everything is all about worry without any control. The second type, commonly known as generalized anxiety disorder, paints a better picture of the chaotic psychic environment.

This categorization also involves various factors that cause anxiety. Many biological theories focus on neural chemical imbalances, such as reduced amounts of serotonin or gamma-aminobutyric acid (GABA), that might account for what is under investigation. Such imbalances are believed to disrupt the balance of the emotional regulation system and make individuals react with higher levels of anxiety or unease to stimuli. Meanwhile, cognitive frameworks stress that maladaptive thinking contributes to the spreading of worries. This could fundamentally change an individual's emotional map in terms of leaning towards fearful thinking about what would be wrong or overestimating danger. In turn, the conditions of the surrounding environment also define the framework of this psychic environment. Trauma, perennial pressure, and inadequate social support could weaken the resilience of the mind, leading to a higher vulnerability to anxiety. Furthermore, numerous influences in the cultural setting are evident. In some countries, people might struggle silently with themselves when it becomes socially undesirable to express themselves publicly or talk about matters relating to mental health.

In addition to these categorizations, the causes of anxiety continue to include a variety of factors. Biological theories often point to neurochemical imbalances, mainly involving neurotransmitters like serotonin and gamma-aminobutyric acid (GABA), as the cause of the condition being studied. These imbalances, which are thought to throw off the homeostasis of the system that regulates emotions, cause people to react to stimuli with increased degrees of anxiety or apprehension. Concurrently, cognitive frameworks place a strong emphasis on the role that maladaptive thinking processes play in the dissemination of worry. An inclination toward thinking about the worst-case scenario or a tendency to exaggerate perceived danger, for example, has the potential to radically transform an individual's emotional landscape. The circumstances in the immediate environment also influence the shapes of this psychic landscape. The resilience of the mind may be weakened, and as a result, it can become more prone to anxiety due to traumatic experiences, persistent pressures, or simply a lack of proper social support. In addition, the cultural settings exert a considerable amount of influence. When it is socially unacceptable to express one self or to talk about issues related to mental health, people in certain countries may struggle in silence with the turmoil that is occurring inside of them, which may make their pain much worse.

Revealing Depression's Shadows

When one begins to investigate the human emotional environment, one cannot ignore the great weight that development places on the mind. It seems as if a deep mist that cannot be penetrated has settled over the mind, obstructing one's view of the bright brilliance of purity and optimism. The profound and all-encompassing shadows cast by development have a significant impact on a person's thoughts, behaviors, and very being as an essential being. It is necessary to have a sophisticated knowledge of the phenomenon before entering this domain. This is a step toward extinguishing the darkness and revealing the pathways of one's inner being. At the same time, it is really necessary to define exactly what it is that constitutes development. In contrast to transitory sorrow or momentary melancholy, depression is a condition that lasts for a longer period and is characterized by a malaise that suffocates the soul for protracted periods. Symptoms may vary from a strong feeling of despair, anhedonia, which is the loss of pleasure in previously pleasurable things, to more somatic concerns such as unremitting tiredness or sleep disorders. Anxiety and depression are two of the most common mental health conditions. It would seem that social factors contribute to the development of depression. On a physiological level, one often runs across conclusions regarding neurotransmitters such as dopamine, serotonin, and norepinephrine. When the delicate balance between them is increased, an individual's susceptibility to mood dysregulation increases. In addition to neurochemistry, genetics has emerged as a key participant in this debate. Depression runs in families and may frequently cause subsequent generations to have similar emotional difficulties. Furthermore, the narrative goes beyond the realm of biology. The psychological and interpersonal aspects are just as important, if not more so. One might fall into the chasms of decay after experiencing things such as boredom, prolonged adverse effects, or traumatic events. Additionally, the management and experience of sadness are both influenced by the circumstances and paradigms of society and culture. The weight of depression is even even prevalent in some cultures, where stoicism becomes valued and emotional weaknesses are stigmatized, making the condition much more difficult to deal with. Despite the daily appearance of the environment, one must not lose sight of the fact that there is room for development. Those who are caught in the shadows of despair might find glimmers of hope via therapeutic techniques, which are analogous to rays of the sun shining through a dark canopy. Individuals who participate in cognitive-behavioral therapy, for example, gain the ability to confront and reconstruct maladaptive thinking, thus increasing their awareness of cognitive distortions. On the other hand, psychodynamic treatments probe into the depths of the unconscious, uncovering prior traumatic experiences as well as issues that have not been addressed. In addition to consultation therapy, the field of pharmacology may also provide relief. Antidepressant medications are effective in reducing depression symptoms for many people, even though there is some controversy around their use. These pharmacological medicines, which often depend on neurotransmitter systems, have the potential to serve as lighthouses, leading people away from the dark seas of depression. The role of one's community and society in providing support is and will continue to be an equally crucial component of this path to enlightenment. An understanding friend, a sympathetic family member, or even a supportive community organization might function as torchbearers for a chosen person, leading them towards the light and helping them overcome their condition. To be successful in this endeavor, social efforts must be concentrated on de-stigmatizing mental illness, expanding access to treatment, and cultivating a society that is accepting of all people.

Mind-Body Methods for Stress Reduction

When navigating the landscape of therapeutic modalities, cognitive-behavioral therapy (also known as CBT) emerges as a leader, especially in regard to its ability to alleviate psychological suffering. This strategy, which is based on the interaction that occurs between cognition and behavior, makes an effort to transform the patterns of the psyche, with the goals of reducing discomfort and enhancing well-being as a result. In order to improve its effectiveness, one must invest in its fundamental concepts, procedures, and the practical consequences it has for reducing emotional anguish. First and foremost, in order to explain the foundations of CBT, it is necessary to acknowledge the essential practice, which states that one's thoughts impact their emotions and, as a result, their actions. The domain of cognition covers the ideas, beliefs, and perceptions that people have about themselves, their surroundings, and the possible futures that lie ahead of them. Catastrophizing and thinking in black are two examples of maladaptive cognitions that may be the root cause of emotional disturbances such as anxiety and hopelessness. Cognitive distortions are another word for maladaptive cognitions. Within the framework of this paradigm, cognitive behavioral therapy (CBT) postulates that one may have a beneficial ripple effect on emotions and actions by altering emotional cognitions. For instance, a person who holds the view that "I am inherently inept" is more likely to experience emotions of worthlessness consistently. The goal of cognitive behavioral therapy (CBT) is to bring about a more balanced emotional state by questioning and altering this thought. CBT's approach is characterized by a variety of approaches, tactics, and methods. The process of cognitive reorganization is one of the most famous methods. During this phase of therapy, the therapist works in conjunction with the client to recognize distorted views, question the reality of those thoughts, and finally develop more flexible ways of thinking. Another effective method is known as behavioral activation, and it encourages patients to take part in satisfying activities in order to break the cycle of hopelessness and passivity that is often associated with diseases such as depression. It is important to highlight exposure treatment as a subfield of cognitive behavioral therapy (CBT). This method is most often used in the treatment of phobic disorders as well as post-traumatic stress disorder. It includes subjecting a person to fear-inducing stimuli in a slow and progressive manner, with the goal of acclimating them to the stimuli and lowering their level of anxiety over time. Individuals are able to take control of their lives and lessen the impact of their worries when they face the cause of their suffering rather than run away from it. In addition, the use of cognitive behavioral therapy in real life may be used with a wide range of people. Because of its organized and goal-oriented character, it is especially useful for those who are looking for real solutions and results. CBT's procedures have shown exceptional flexibility and efficacy when used with a wide range of patients, from youngsters coping with anxiety to adults experiencing depressive episodes. However, similar to other forms of therapeutic intervention, cognitive behavioral therapy (CBT) is not immune to criticism. By putting the majority of its emphasis on cognitive processes, some contend that it oversimplifies simplifies complicated emotional disorders. In response to this criticism, supporters of CBT highlight the dynamic character of the field, pointing out that recent offshoots of the technique, such as mindfulness-based cognitive therapy, have begun adding meditative activities in order to address patients' worries.

Explaining Neurochemical Imbalances

In the complicated field of neuroscience, discussions often meander their way to the delicate balance of chemicals that exist inside the human brain. These molecules, which are known as neurotransmitters, play an essential role as messengers, ensuring that billions of neurons can communicate with one another without any disruptions. The disruption of this precarious equilibrium, on the other hand, may pave the way for a wide variety of mental and physical illnesses. In order to fully comprehend the tremendous effects that neurochemical imbalances might have, it is necessary to conduct in-depth research.

Neurotransmitters, despite the fact that they occupy such a minute amount of space in our bodies, have a colossal impact on every feeling, thought, and deed that we experience. These substances are responsible for navigating the intricate brain networks and ensuring that messages are properly sent from one cell to the next. The role of serotonin as a mood stabilizer is often lauded. On the other hand, dopamine is intimately connected to the pleasure and reward processes in the brain. In its action as an inhibitor, GABA ensures that the excitability of neurons is kept under control.

The accumulation of severe psychological symptoms may be the end result of a disruption in the normal amounts of these neurotransmitters. For example, researchers have shown a correlation between low serotonin levels and sad feelings. On the other side, an overactive dopamine activity has been postulated to be a factor to illnesses such as schizophrenia. Alterations in the activity of the neurotransmitter GABA have been hypothesized to be the cause of various anxiety disorders. When one considers the etiological features, one comes to the conclusion that the causes of these imbalances stem from a variety of different places. The blueprint of our genes, which is passed down through the generations, may make us more susceptible to certain neurochemical patterns.

Our neurochemical milieu is also shaped by the interactions with our environments. Our neurochemical equilibrium may get disrupted when we are subjected to chronic stress, grief, or simply continuous exposure to unpleasant conditions. In addition, some physiological conditions, such as thyroid diseases or brain traumas, have the potential to wreak havoc on the delicate balance of our neurotransmitters. The diagnosis of these abnormalities is a difficult problem. Direct measurement is still difficult to achieve.

Instead, doctors often depend on clinical presentations to make their diagnoses. Even while they do not directly measure neurotransmitters, modern imaging methods give insights into brain activity, which might provide possible indications regarding underlying imbalances. To correct these inequalities, a multipronged strategy is required to be implemented. Modulating the activity of neurotransmitters is the goal of pharmacological therapies like as antidepressants and antipsychotics, which try to restore the equilibrium that was lost. Even if psychotherapeutic treatments do not directly affect neurotransmitters, they may nonetheless promote brain plasticity and have the ability to correct imbalances over the course of longer periods of time.

Emerging treatments such as neurofeedback, despite the fact that they are still in their infant phases hold the promise of providing patients with some measure of control over the activity that occurs in their brains. Despite the fact that the narrative of neurochemical imbalances has had a significant impact on the therapies used in psychiatry, it has not been exempt from criticism. Opponents of this approach contend that it simplifies a too complex phenomenon, namely the multiple character of psychiatric diseases. In addition, while drugs might provide relief, they do not come without their baggage in the form of possible withdrawal symptoms or adverse effects. In the enormous tapestry that is neuroscience, the section on neurochemical imbalances continues to be one of the most interesting and important parts. It provides a prism through which to study the interaction between biology and psychology, as well as the relationship between neurons and feelings. As researchers explore further into this field, there is reason to maintain optimism that they will uncover more complex insights and develop effective solutions that will ensure the physical and mental health of all people.

Explaining Neurochemical Imbalances

The field of pharmacological therapies has maintained its position at the front of medical innovation in today's quickly changing world. These therapies, which are filled to the brim with limitless potential, promise a significant reshaping of the treatment techniques that are now available. Historically, the expertise of this profession was shown via pharmaceuticals that changed people's lives. These treatments were used to treat anything from bacterial infections to chronic metabolic diseases. It is impossible to avoid coming awestruck by the immense advancements made, particularly in more recent eras. Targeted treatments are a product of in-depth knowledge of molecular biology, which has led to their development.

These technological wonders are intended to have a laser-like focus on certain chemical targets. This improved precision not only increases the effectiveness of the treatment, but it also reduces the severity of any systemic side effects. As we get further into the field of pharmacology, we reach the realm of biological therapies. These entities, having beginnings that are anchored in live beings, typically exhibit superiority in specificity when compared to their conventional counterparts.

 This is because living organisms have more complex structures. These kinds of drugs have the potential to completely

revolutionize treatment, in particular for diseases like cancer and autoimmune disorders. The idea of customized medicine shines even more light on the many opportunities that exist within this sector. The fact that medicines may now be tailored to an individual's genetic blueprints is a credit to the development of medicine. These kinds of treatments anticipate optimal results since they make it their mission to tailor the therapy to the specific physiological architecture of each patient.

However, the path toward pharmaceutical progress is not one that is free of obscurities. Even after extensive testing, it is possible that unanticipated negative medication reactions may occur.

These events passionately argue for unwavering monitoring after the market has already closed. In addition, the development of novel treatments is sometimes accompanied by significant additional financial obligations. This monetary might raise issues about equal access, in particular for people who live in economically limited places of the world. Antimicrobial resistance is one of the the concerns that shines out in a very striking way. This enormous risk, which was brought about by improper use of antibiotics and excessive prescription of them, compels the need of international cooperation. Even outside of the sphere of science, ethical muck may sometimes be found. Arguments may get heated when decisions concerning access are being made, particularly for innovative restricted therapies.

In addition, the commercialization of research may sometimes swing the pendulum away from the wellbeing of patients and toward financial rewards.

Social networks provide stability in times of stress

Throughout the long annals of human history, we have been confronted with an endless variety of obstacles that have repeatedly put our mettle to the test. However, one fact that has stood the test of time is that the stable cornerstones of our society are our social networks, which are comprised of a nuanced mix of family relationships, friendships, and community affiliations. These ties, some of which are more concrete than others, serve as beacons that lead us safely across the turbulent seas of anxiety and unpredictability.

Social networks are illustrative of the underlying desire for connection that all humans have, from the time when ancient tribes gathered around roaring fires to tell stories to the present day when instant digital communications are sent across international borders. Simply putting one's concerns and unanswered questions into words might bring about a significant sense of comfort. When the concerns of one person are heard by another who is sympathetic, it helps to cultivate a feeling of shared humanity.

This emotional communion frequently serves as a barrier against excessive stress, anchoring people in shared experience and mutual comprehension of one another's perspectives. The relevance of group dynamics in our lives is predicated on the fact that we evolved to become social beings. The essence of community is intricately woven into the very fabric of human society as well as biological processes. When under pressure, it's important to talk about the emotional turmoil you're going through and find people who can empathize with you.

According to some studies, healthy social relationships may even lower cortisol levels and lessen the impact of stress on a person's body. This physiological balance ultimately instills a sense of tranquility and centeredness, which helps to strengthen the spirit against disturbances from the outside world. The strength of communal solidarity is shown when it is put to the test by shared challenges, such as the wrath of nature or turbulent sociopolitical conditions. Communities often exhibit a one-of-a-kind alchemy by fusing their strengths and resources, which exemplifies the concept of collective resilience. Within this intricate web of intertwined struggles, people regularly come face to face with exemplars who have triumphed over problems of a like kind. When one studies the methods that they have used to achieve success in the past, not only does one get useful insights, but one also acquires a sense of optimism and resolve.

Traditional forms of social networks have had their scope expanded as a result of the advent of the digital age. Platforms that link people on different continents have given rise to extensive communities all around the world. These online havens are flourishing as hubs of support, information sharing, and collective activism just as the world outside them is becoming more turbulent. However, despite the many advantages offered by the digital environment, extreme care is still required while navigating it.

In its shadows, misinformation, and digital malevolence lurk, highlighting the need of exercising discernment and engaging in prudent activity. The unexpected nature of life's stage means that stress and difficulties are always there as co-actors. Nevertheless, a sense of security may be attained via the ever-present existence of social networks, which are throbbing with empathy, collective power, and shared knowledge. One may navigate the uneven terrains of life with strength, elegance, and a profound feeling of belonging if one places value on these relationships and works to cultivate them.

Depressive State History

The emotional landscapes of humans have always fluctuated, and this pattern may be seen throughout the annals of history. The contrast between light and dark in our minds allows us to express both the brightest of pleasures and the darkest of grief. Among them, depressed moods, which may be described as a deep sorrow or desolation that goes beyond simple sadness, have been brought up on several occasions. As we go across the eras of history, we can see that people's views, interpretations, and approaches to treating depressed conditions show a mosaic of human knowledge and the development of society and culture. Emotional disturbances were often given meaning by ancient cultures by looking at them through the lens of spirituality or the supernatural. In the papyrus scrolls that they had, the

Egyptians spoke of symptoms that were similar to depression. They believed that hostile deities or possession were to blame for these disorders. The performance of rituals, the utterance of invocations, and the donning of amulets were often components of remedies. Similarly, the ancient Greeks, who were known for their deep knowledge, hypothesized about the impact of the body's natural humors. It was thought that an abundance of black bile was the root cause of the melancholy condition. Hippocrates and, later, Galen, both renowned doctors, offered many therapies for their patients, ranging from dietary adjustments to bloodletting. In the Middle Ages, when religious zeal dominated society, many believed that melancholy moods were reflections of moral shortcomings or tests from God. A spiritual listlessness known as "acedia" is mentioned sporadically in monastic texts. It was a fight between faith and despair for many people, with the latter frequently being attributed to forces from the demonic realm.

Exorcisms, as well as acts of prayer and penance, were among the most common types of treatment used during this time period. The Renaissance and the Enlightenment eras marked the beginning of a transition, which prompted the conversation to gradually move toward a more humanistic and medical viewpoint. The writings of illustrious individuals like Robert Burton, such as his magnum opus "The Anatomy of Melancholy," presented detailed insights into the plethora of elements that are associated with the illness. He combined the existing medical knowledge of the time with his observations and came to the conclusion that social pressures, love, and even economic reasons may all contribute to a person's descent into melancholy. Long-lasting imprints had been made on the human mind by the time the industrial revolution, urbanization, and rapid social upheaval occurred in the 19th century. The clinical connotations of the word "melancholia" became more prevalent.

Psychoanalytical interpretations were offered for depressed moods about the same time that renowned thinkers such as Sigmund Freud started to investigate the complexities of the mind. The establishment of asylums heralded the beginning of institutional treatment for mental illnesses; nonetheless, these early facilities were notorious for their appalling living conditions. throughout both the knowledge of and approaches to the treatment of depression, seismic developments occurred throughout the 20th century. The World Wars, with their significant psychological effects, required concentrated attention on the mental health of troops, which resulted in the birth of terminology like "shell shock." Both the field of psychiatry and the field of psychology were flourishing at the same time. Emerging biological hypotheses focused on neurotransmitter abnormalities as the root of the problem. Antidepressants first appeared in the latter part of the 20th century, ushering in a new age of pharmaceutical treatments. Drugs such as Prozac were among the first of their kind. A more comprehensive knowledge of depressed moods is possible because to the kaleidoscope of technical developments that have occurred in modern times. The integration of neuroscience, genetics, and psychology yields extensive new understandings. There is a wide variety of treatment options available, ranging from cognitive behavioral therapy and sophisticated pharmaceutical regimens to neuromodulation treatments and the like. In conclusion, the voyage through history sheds light on the ever-evolving fabric of human thinking in relation to depressed conditions. Our perspectives have been profoundly altered, going from spiritual interpretations to rigorous scientific evaluations, and everywhere in between. Nevertheless, the fundamental purpose continues to be the same: the search for comprehension, empathy, and relief from the terrible despair that may at times settle over the human soul. As we go on, equipped with the knowledge of yesterday and the instruments of today, the optimism that the future will be brighter and more compassionate for individuals who are entangled in the tendrils of despair continues to exist.

Nontraditional Therapies

Within the expansive landscape that is healthcare, conventional medical procedures have always held the position of center stage. These techniques, which have their origins in empirical research, clinical trials, and methodological rigor, have been crucial in forming our knowledge of illness, health, and treatment paradigms. However, emanating from this central pillar are a plethora of alternative treatments, each of which has a distinctive strategy for promoting health and well-being. These alternative treatments, which often draw their motivation from age-old knowledge, the natural world, or fresh points of view, provide fascinating alternatives to the norm. The field of complementary and alternative medicine is enormous, and it encompasses a wide variety of treatment modalities.

These modalities, which often deviate from the practices associated with allopathy, combine elements of art, science, custom, and creativity. Alternative treatments provide comprehensive views on health, ranging from the hands-on procedures used in chiropractic therapy to the energy harmonization that is accomplished via Reiki. Traditional Chinese Medicine (also known as TCM) is responsible for the development of one of the first kinds of alternative medicines.

Traditional Chinese Medicine (TCM) is a practice that dates back thousands of years and combines acupuncture, herbal medicine, cupping treatment, and qigong. The idea of Qi, which refers to the flow of vital energy, is essential to this practice. TCM adherents believe that restoring the body's natural balance may be accomplished by bringing this flow into harmony, which in turn promotes health and protects against sickness. Ayurveda, which originated on the Indian subcontinent, is yet another rich trove of traditional medicinal practices. Ayurveda places an emphasis on balance because it views the human body as a confluence of forces known as "doshas."

It provides cleansing, regeneration, and a road to overall well-being by means of herbal treatments, dietary guidance, and activities such as Panchakarma. Although techniques such as Traditional Chinese Medicine (TCM) and Ayurveda have been around for a long time and have historical origins, some alternative treatments have just lately come into existence and draw upon contemporary understandings or the merging of many cultures. For example, chiropractic treatment concentrates on the musculoskeletal system, and more specifically on the spine. Chiropractors think that they may improve nerve function and general health by correcting the vertebrae in the body when they are out of alignment. Homeopathy is yet another well-known kind of alternative medicine, and it is predicated on the idea that "like cures like."

The goal of homeopathy is to activate the body's natural healing response by giving very diluted amounts of chemicals that, if taken in greater quantities, would cause symptoms of the condition being treated. Beyond this, there is a whole universe of treatments that are based on energy. The Japanese practice of Reiki is based on the idea that one may heal, relax, and rebalance themselves by channeling universal life force energy. In a similar vein, methods like as Theta Healing and Quantum Touch use meditation and concentrated intention to bring about healing on all levels, including the physical, the emotional, and the spiritual. In the world of medicine, the question of whether or not alternative treatments really work is one that often sparks heated discussion. Skeptics want to see more empirical data, despite the fact that there are certain patients and practitioners who swear by the effects. It is essential to recognize the duality that exists here. Even though there are numerous anecdotal success stories associated with alternative medicines, formal scientific research are often hard to come by. Undoubtedly, though, there is a growing interest all around the world in these treatments. Alternative treatments are gaining popularity as a growing number of people look for natural, holistic, and individualized approaches to their health and wellness. They often have fewer adverse effects, place a greater emphasis on prevention, and foster a more deep feeling of well-being in the patient.

Incorporating complementary and alternative treatments does not require abandoning conventional treatment approaches. On the other hand, a synergistic approach, sometimes known as 'integrative medicine,' is becoming more popular. This strategy combines the advantages of both approaches, which results in holistic treatment for the patient.

Culture's Transformation from Stigma to Acceptance

Since the beginning of time, society as a whole has been in charge of wielding the two-sided sword of acceptance and rejection. Certain attitudes, ways of having, and identities have, at various times and in a variety of eras, been shunned, labeled as taboo, or covered in stigma. However, the unstoppable march of time, along with evolving viewpoints, has caused society's lens to progressively change from attitudes that exclude others to those that embrace a wider range of people and ideas.

This story sheds light on the development of social perspectives, following the progression from exclusion to inclusion along the way. Throughout history, a multitude of different cultures have entrenched rigorous frameworks that outline what is considered normal and what is considered abnormal. These frames, which were shaped by religious dogmas, conventional standards, and often dread of the unexpected, threw shadows over everything that did not correspond to the expectations. Many subjects, including diseases like leprosy and mental health disorders as well as varied sexual orientations, were kept in the shadows, ignored, or given a negative connotation. Diseases, particularly those that were poorly understood at the time, were thought to be divine punishments or curses in many ancient cultures. People who were affected by the disease were often avoided, deported, or covered in shame.

This exclusionary strategy was not just used for situations related to health. Strong opposition was met by personal identities, in particular those that deviated from the heteronormative spectrum. In many different societies, homosexuality was seen as sinful and subject to punishment or as something that required "correction." In spite of this gloomy climate of prejudice, the seeds of transformation were planted here and there here and there. Progressive intellectuals, artists, and philosophers have sometimes been known to question established conventions.

Even if their voices were muted in comparison to others of their day, the spirit of acceptance, understanding, and compassion resonated through them. The Age of Enlightenment was a time that saw a profound shift in the way that society perceived things. Many long-established dogmas were called into question as the importance of reason, scientific discovery, and individual rights came to the fore. In the past, mental diseases were seen through the lens of dread and superstition. However, recently, they have started to be regarded as medical problems. In their early stages, the disciplines of psychology and psychiatry sought, rather than avoided, the study of disorders like these. The 20th century saw an increase in the number of social movements and civil rights fights. Together, activists, intellectuals, and people who had been negatively impacted by social stigmas challenged the stigmas head-on.

For example, members of the LGBTQ+ community have courageously fought biases while promoting equal rights, recognition, and respect. In the second half of the 20th century, significant advances were made in a variety of areas, including the legalization of homosexuality in a number of countries and wider acceptance of a wide range of gender identities. Concurrently, the hitherto taboo subject of mental health has emerged as a central issue of discussion in the public sphere. People in the public eye, including celebrities and prominent figures, as well as average citizens, started talking about their challenges, refuting misunderstandings and normalizing conversations about mental health. The arrival of the internet era in the 21st century greatly magnified the voices of those who advocated for acceptance of many identities.

Havens have been offered in the form of social media platforms, blogs, and online communities for those who were previously ostracized. Stories were spoken, support was gathered, and worldwide initiatives were started, all with the goal of making society more welcoming to people of all identities and backgrounds.

On the other hand, the path from stigma to acceptance is not uniform nor necessarily a linear one. Even in this day and age, there are still isolated cases of discrimination. There are still elements inside certain nations and communities that hold traditional values and beliefs. Despite this, the overall trend seems to be heading in the right direction. Initiatives at the grassroots level, educational programs, and legislative changes are always pushing the edge and campaigning for wider acceptance of their respective causes.

Anxious Responses' Biology

Concerning the field of biological research, anxiety continues to be a mystery. Even though there are a lot of hypotheses about where it came from, nobody really knows. Without a shadow of a doubt, one of the most fundamental aspects of the human experience is that of anxiety. This emotional reaction has been with Homo sapiens throughout the epochs, as may be deduced through an astute examination of historical evidence. Nevertheless, why? What kinds of biological processes are responsible for these bothersome feelings? The brain is the source of worry at its most fundamental level. The amygdala, which is buried deep inside the architecture of the brain, plays an essential part. This almond-shaped thing gives people warnings about possible dangers in their environment. An excessive activation of this region is typically associated with an increased level of apprehension. The hippocampus is located right next to the amygdala in the brain. In addition to its role in memory and cognition, its interaction with the amygdala continues to be crucial. A link between these two areas that is poorly controlled has been shown in a significant number of studies to be a major contributor to anxiety disorders. The endocrine system is also intertwined with this story in several ways. Cortisol is a hormone that is linked to stress, and it is produced by glands called the adrenals, which sit above the kidneys. In humans, persistent anxiety is the result of having cortisol levels that are chronically high. This endocrine-anxiety nexus sheds light on why those who are exposed to continuous stress are more likely to suffer from anxiety disorders. Neurotransmitters, crucial substances found in our brains, are responsible for mood regulation. GABA, or gamma-aminobutyric acid, and serotonin, two of the most important neurotransmitters, are responsible for maintaining emotional balance. Feelings of unease might be brought on by shifts in their concentrations. Inhibiting excitable neural activity is what GABA does, while serotonin is what promotes emotions of well-being. Therefore, worry often follows in its wake whenever there is an imbalance. Genetics, a relatively new but rapidly developing discipline, provides some interesting hints. Certain people, as a result of their genetic make-up, have a predisposition to suffer from anxiety problems. Researchers believe that some gene alterations could make a person more susceptible to developing certain diseases. As a result, genetics adds yet another dimension to this multidimensional problem.

How to Navigate Therapeutic Interventions

Even though we often think of sleep as a nightly escape into oblivion, the truth is that it has enormous consequences for the emotional landscape we leave each day. It is only when one is deprived of peaceful sleep that one is forced to confront the tremendous importance of having had such sleep. Nights that are filled with restlessness often herald in days that are loaded with emotional instability. The prefrontal cortex emerges as a key role when investigating the link between sleep and mood as it relates to the prefrontal cortex. This brain area is tasked with a pantheon of duties, and when it is denied its quota of rest, it discovers that its effectiveness is lessened. One of its primary responsibilities, emotional regulation, is impaired when an individual does not get enough sleep. This deficiency sheds light on the emotional upheavals that might be brought on by a sleepless night. The amygdala, which is known as the "bastion of emotional processing," is located near the aforementioned area and exhibits some fascinating patterns. People who are deprived of the blessing of sleep have an increased level of responsiveness. This heightened activity within the amygdala drives people into a stormy emotional world; yet, since the prefrontal cortex is not there to offer its regular moderating function, this moderating influence is absent. When in such a mindset, even the most routine of events might provoke excessive emotional reactions. When one delves into the world of endocrinology, one discovers the complex relationship that exists between sleep and hormones. Cortisol, which is sometimes referred to be the hormone that heralds the arrival of stress, demonstrates a great sensitivity to one's sleeping habits. When you wake up after a restorative sleep, your cortisol levels will be lower than when you went to sleep, and this will help you have an emotionally balanced day. On the other hand, nights that are disrupted by sleep interruptions lead to higher cortisol concentrations, which plants the seeds for emotional instability. A complicated dance exists between melatonin, sometimes known as the "happy chemical," and serotonin, also known as the "chemical of contentment." The transformation of the amino acid tryptophan into the neurotransmitter serotonin takes place throughout the nighttime hours, especially during the deeper stages. A lack of sleep might thus stifle this synthesis, which raises the possibility of experiencing mood problems. In the dreamworld, rapid eye movement (REM) sleep, which is characterized by very vivid dreams, manifests as an emotional tonic. In the nighttime theater of dreams, one might see a one-of-a-kind alchemy taking place as a result of one's emotional experiences. When recalled in alertness, these memories no longer have the same potency since they were processed over the night and became less intimidating as a result. It is imperative that one does not circumvent the circadian rhythm, since this natural timekeeper is responsible for coordinating a wide variety of physiological functions.

The management of mood is included within its expansive scope of influence. Mood swings are the outward manifestation of disruptions in this cycle, which are often the result of irregular sleep patterns. Therefore, synchronizing one's sleep pattern with this rhythm presents itself as a tactic that is of the utmost importance for maintaining one's mental health.

Linking and Causing Dietary Influences

A person's diet, which is like a tapestry made up of a variety of different materials and nutrients, has a tremendous influence on their health and well-being. The complex dynamic that exists between the things that one puts into their body and the subsequential consequences that those things have on the body has been the focus of a great deal of study. Although it is abundantly clear that nutrition plays an important part in one's overall health, separating the factors that are just correlational from those that are really causal continues to be a challenging endeavor. Over the course of the last few decades, there has been an exploration of epistemological history in the published scientific literature. Each of these studies sheds light on possible links between dietary patterns and health consequences. However, one must proceed with caution; it is not always the case that a correlation indicates a causal relationship. People who eat a diet that is rich in fruits and vegetables may have a lower chance of developing a number of different illnesses, according to the findings of a number of research studies. Although this seems to be helpful, it is essential to ask the following question: Does the eating of these foods directly contribute to improved health, or are there other factors at play that may be confusing the issue? Let us continue to explore this miracle to its fullest extent.

Consider, for instance, the purported advantages of consuming a diet rich in olive oil, lentils, and seafood. This diet is known as the medieval diet. Studies that are based on observations exhibit its charms and associate it with a decreased risk of cardiovascular diseases. However, as one digs further into the specifics, one finds that there are certain ambiguities. People who adhere to such a diet could also participate in regular physical exercise, refrain from smoking, or maintain strong social relationships, all of which contribute to a healthy lifestyle in and of themselves. Therefore, would it be accurate to say that the person itself is the only factor responsible for their benefits? Randomized controlled trials, often known as RCTs, are the research industry's gold standard.

Their purpose is to solve problems like these. They reduce the possibility of confounding factors by using random allocation, which provides a sharper lens through which to examine the relationship between the two variables. Researchers have been able to confirm the detrimental effects of trans fats on heart health by using randomized controlled trials (RCTs), displaying not only a correlation but actual causation in the process. Furthermore, the study surrounding the gut microbiota, which is still in its infancy, provides some intriguing new perspectives. It would seem that diet has a significant impact on this microbial population, which in turn modifies a wide variety of elements of one's health, ranging from digestion to inflammation and even mood. A direct chain of causation may be found here.

For example, diets that are high in fiber create an environment in the gut that is conducive to the growth of good bacteria. These bacteria then convert the fibers into short-chain fatty acids, which have an anti-inflammatory impact. On the other hand, there is an opposing viewpoint to this account. Not all dietary variables contribute to a healthy lifestyle. Consuming an excessive amount of processed sugars, for instance, has been linked to a wide variety of diseases, including metabolic syndrome and cognitive impairment. Although early studies suggested that these were just correlations, there is now a growing body of research that suggests that there may be a more sinister and causal link. It would seem that consuming an excessive amount of sugar might cause insulin resistance and promote inflammation, laying the groundwork for the development of chronic illnesses.

The function of micronutrients is another aspect that demands some attention and initiative. Even though they are only needed in very minute quantities, trace elements have a significant impact on one's overall health. Iron, for example, is an essential component in the process of oxygen transport. Its deficiency does not only correlate with fatigue; rather, it causes weakness by making it more difficult for the body to produce hemoglobin.

Exercise as a Cure for the Blues?

In the annals of human history, physical exercise was seen as an essential component of the day-to-day lives of people. Moving was not an option but rather a must for everything early humans did, from hunting and gathering to cultivating the land. A startling shift becomes apparent as one jumps in time for the perfect day. The advent of new technologies has contributed to the rise of secularism, which in turn has led to the emergence of a wide variety of illnesses. In light of all of this, it is natural to wonder whether or not engaging in physical exercise may provide a cure-all for the ubiquitous malaise that afflicts contemporary society. The malaise, which is often accompanied by feelings of discomfort, wheariness, and depression, has its origins in a wide variety of factors. The origins of this pain are still murky, but they likely have something to do with the mental and physiological stresses that come with continuous living. However, in the middle of all of this complexity, there is one thing that stands out as a ray of hope: physical exercise. The field of neuroscience is full of fascinating discoveries and lessons to be learned. Endorphins are released into the bloodstream when a person engages in physical activity of any kind, whether it is a leisurely stroll or an intense exercise. These neurotransmitters are responsible for the euphoric emotions that people experience, which are also known as the 'runner's high.' They have dubbed the 'feel-good' hormones. The effects of these substances on mood are supported by a substantial body of scientific research, which goes beyond anecdotal evidence alone. As a result, physical exercise instantly combats the emotions of disease and unease because it stimulates the production of endorphins. As one moves further into the world of the brain, one is compelled to consider the role that physical activity plays in the process of neurogenesis, particularly in the hippocampus. The hippocampus, which is critical to learning and memory, is a region of the brain that is especially susceptible to the impacts of physical activity.

The formation of new neurons in this area is encouraged by consistent physical exercise, which in turn improves cognitive capabilities. As a direct consequence of this, the mental haze and sluggishness that are classic symptoms of malaise are lifted. There is no question that regular physical exercise has positive effects on cardiovascular health at a systemic level. Some of the many benefits include improved cardiac output, increased oxygenation, and efficient nutrition delivery. There are many more benefits. Every time the heart beats, a burst of energy is sent through the body, which energizes every cell in the process.

This physiological regulation, in turn, fights against the physical weakness that often comes along with malaise. The advantages to your musculoskeletal system are many as well. A feeling of grounding may be achieved by actively contracting one's muscles, extending one's ligaments, and moving one's joints. Individuals are rooted in the here and now as a result of the connection that is established between them and their physical bodies via their participation in kinematic engagement. This kind of awareness, which is often the result of engaging in physical exercise, is an effective treatment for the existential disquiet that is typical of malaise. In addition to this, the field of endocrinology provides more clarification on this matter. The levels of sexual hormones, including cortisol, which is known as the stress hormone, may be altered by engaging in physical exercise. Exercise significantly lowers levels of stress by reducing the release of cortisol, making it an effective weapon against one of the causes of malaise. Furthermore, it is of the utmost importance to sound a note of warning.

Although engaging in physical exercise proves to be a powerful ally in the fight against malaise, it is not a cure-all. Important aspects include individual differences, the kind and level of exercise performed, as well as lifestyle factors that are consistent with exercise. For some, the advantages may manifest themselves in an obvious and immediate manner, while for others, they may be more subtle. It is crucial to approach this task with a balanced perspective, understanding its enormous promise while also appreciating the constraints it imposes.

Physical Activity: Anti-Malaise

In today's world, there is a profound melancholy that has spread across the fabric of our society. People who allow themselves to become trapped in secondary routines typically languish. In spite of this, there is a powerful cure to depression that is sometimes overlooked, and that is engaging in physical activity.

unlocks a multi-faceted technique that offers a variety of benefits, both physiological and psychological, while engaging in the movement of our bodies. A generalized sense of disquiet or discomfort is what is meant when we talk about malaise. The hazy quality of it might originate from a wide variety of factors, such as boredom brought on by performing routine duties or the existential death caused by the practices of modern life. Nevertheless, it becomes clear that there is one practice that cannot be disputed: Engaging in physical exercise acts as a defense mechanism against the feeling of unease. This activity comprises any physiological movement produced by skeletal muscles that enhances the endurance of exercise and should not be confused with simple exercise. Rehabilitation can be achieved by activities as seemingly inconsequential as standing still, as well as through walking and dancing. From a physiological point of view, engaging in physical exercise strengthens the internal systems of the body. There is a significant improvement in the evolution of the cardiovascular system. When working together, the heart and lungs are able to carry oxygen more effectively. Additionally, improvements can be shown in both physical strength and flexibility. The improvement of one's immunization system should be the ultimate goal of such upgrades. As a direct consequence of this, individuals have a strong resistance to infections, resulting in fewer cases of disease.

In addition to the area of simple physiology, there are unquestionable benefits for the mind. Benefits are many for one's mental health, which in this day and age is of the utmost importance. Endorphins, sometimes known as "feel-good" chemicals, are released into the bloodstream by the brain as a result of engaging in physical activity. These chemicals have analgesic and mood-enhancing effects, making them naturally occurring analgesics. As a direct result of this, the dark clouds of despair and anxiety begin to lift, and they are succeeded by a radiant halo of positivity and resilience. However, when extolling the merits of exercise, one must proceed with extreme caution. If you practice physical exercise in a way that is universally applicable, you run the risk of unintentionally ignoring the specific requirements and constraints of universal people. Because of this, customization is still quite important. It is necessary to take into account a number of elements, including the current physical state of the individual, a comprehension of their motivations, and the customization of a routine that strikes a balance between the degree of difficulty and its practicability. In addition, it is important to note that even though physical activity has the potential to be an antidote for malaise, it might not serve as a panacea for everyone. This is something that should be taken into consideration. Those who are battling persistent problems with their mental health require a comprehensive treatment plan that may include, but is not limited to, engaging in physical activity.

Education and advocacy are two of the most important tasks. The introduction of physical education in schools, not as an extracurricular activity but as an essential component, brings with it an abundance of potential benefits. Students have the potential to develop a passion for movement that will last a lifetime if they are exposed to it at an early age. In addition, community caregivers might provide a variety of programs that are geared toward people of all ages, which would ensure that engaging in physically active pursuits is appropriate for everyone. In addition, they believe in innovation. The use of emerging technologies such as virtual reality and augmented reality into existing protocols for physical exercise has the potential to increase participation in those protocols. Individuals may discover that their motivation is increased by gaming the experience, so altering what was once considered a drudgery into an enjoyable quest that they must complete. In order to achieve meaningful transformation, the reconstruction of society is required. Reimagining urban environments, which are frequently fortresses of sectarianism, is necessary. Parks and open spaces that are easily integrated into city designs would encourage citizens to get out and be active. Because cycling and walking are encouraged by infrastructure, residents will be more likely to choose these modes of transportation over driving for shorter distances, which will definitely result in increased mobility throughout the day.

Existential Issues in Depression: A Multifaceted Look

Existential theories hypothesize that people would always look for deeper significance in their lives as well as a sense of purpose and self-worth. When people struggle with existential issues, they may find themselves confronting serious questions about the meaning of life, death, freedom, and loneliness. Within the context of this theoretical paradigm, depressive episodes usually entangle with such concerns, so generating a nexus of psychological anguish.

A cognitive shift is produced as a result of the pervasive illness that is depression. People who are affected by this condition frequently describe feelings of emptiness and a severe lack of significance in their lives. They could get the impression that life is a meaningless existence with no value or purpose to it. As a result of this depressing situation, a number of thoughts come to mind, including "Why am I here?" "What purpose does suffering serve?" and "Will I ever find happiness?" These musings aren't simply the result of a troubled mind wandering aimlessly. Indeed, they have their origins profoundly embedded in existential conundrums.

Existential issues and manic episodes provide an interesting dynamic that might be investigated further as a result of their juxtaposition. Existential therapists, in particular, contend that an individual's encounter with the inherent ambiguities and uncertainties of existence may be the source of melancholy sentiments in that individual. When confronted with such riddles, individuals run the risk of succumbing to an overpowering sense of hopelessness, particularly if they are unable to discover answers that make sense to them.

During bouts of depression, one's preoccupation with the concept of death, which is a primary existential concern, often intensifies. The inevitability of death has the potential to produce paralyzing fear and anxiety. A person suffering from depression may become preoccupied with this finality, which can contribute to feelings of helplessness. In addition, such people may ruminate on the ephemeral quality of existence, which drives them relentlessly towards a gulf of desolation.

In a similar vein, the concept of freedom, which is typically regarded in a favorable light, takes on a solemn tenor when considered in the context of sadness. Not only does "existential freedom" refer to one's own physical autonomy, but also to the limitless opportunities that one is presented with throughout their lifetime. In a strange twist of fate, all of this vast freedom can lead to anxiety. Someone who is already immersed in a cloud of depression may view the overwhelming possibilities as an impossible burden because of how overwhelming they are. Instead of being a source of freedom, choice becomes a source of misery for the individual.

Existential worries are organized into a hierarchy, and loneliness is another one of these pillars. People can experience a severe sense of isolation even when they are surrounded by a large number of other people. This feeling of solitude is likely to become more pronounced during depressed episodes. People might have the impression that they are inherently distinct from one another and that they are confined to their own ideas. A perception such as this might exasperate feelings of isolation, which can further ground a person in hopelessness.

The investigation of meaning, or the absence of it, reveals yet another junction between existential concerns and clinical depression. A well-known psychiatrist by the name of Victor Frankl put forth the hypothesis that a lack of meaning could result in an existential void, also known as a feeling of emptiness. People who are in the throes of depression may struggle fiercely with this void, looking for a glimmer of meaning in a sea of nihilism as they search for a purpose lighthouse.

Therefore, how might different therapy modalities handle the fact that existential worries often go hand in hand with bouts of depression? To begin, it is essential to acknowledge how these things are intertwined. Therapeuts need to be aware that serious existential battles may be raging beneath the surface of a patient's misery. Therapists are able to foster an environment of understanding, empathy, and introspection by simply admitting the challenges their patients face.

Existential therapy, with its focus on personal freedom, responsibility, and the search for meaning, offers a solid foundation for such attempts due to the breadth and depth of its theoretical foundation. It encourages individuals to face the inherent uncertainties that life presents rather than attempting to avoid them. People can begin their journey towards self-awareness and, ultimately, a deeper understanding of their existential issues by engaging in this encounter, which enables them to embark on the journey.

The use of narrative therapy is another approach that shows promise. Individuals are able to infuse their past experiences with new meanings when they are given the opportunity to rewrite the narratives of their lives. This re-authoring has the potential to develop resilience, which in turn enables individuals to manage depressed episodes with newfound enthusiasm.

Genetic Dispositions: Mind Vulnerabilities Mapping

The genetic blueprints of human beings function as the most fundamental kind of maps. They set the stage for the physiological development and tendencies of the organism. Nevertheless, outward appearance is not the only factor to consider. One aspect, which spans the core framework of our cognitive environment, is frequently forgotten about. The purpose of this essay is to shed light on such predispositions and emphasize mental susceptibilities that are associated with genetics.

Throughout human history, nature and nurture have engaged in a constant struggle for preeminence in the process of forming individuals. New research, on the other hand, seem to agree and suggest that both factors have an effect. Particularly, genes do have a significant influence in the process. They write a portion of our mental predispositions, as well as our strengths and, unfortunately, our weaknesses.

Conditions of mental health are one of the most prominent domains in which genes are able to exert their influence and power. In the course of scientific research, linkages have been uncovered between specific genes and an increased likelihood of developing illnesses such as schizophrenia, bipolar disorder, and major depressive disorder. An example of this would be the gene DRD4, which is related with the control of dopamine and may have a correlation with attention deficit hyperactivity disorder. These discoveries give rise to an entirely new mystery. How should members of society view people who carry these genetic markers?

The simple fact that an individual carries a certain genetic marker does not automatically predestine them to acquire the disease that is associated with that marker. It does nothing more than make someone more susceptible. Therefore, one may argue that elements in the environment can change, magnify, or even inhibit the effects of genetic predispositions.

The situation is comparable to that of a garden. If seeds are supposed to reflect genetic predispositions, then the soil, water, and sunlight should be understood to stand in for environmental factors. A seed may have the innate potential to develop into a vigorous plant, but if it is not exposed to adequate sunshine or if the soil it is growing in is poisonous, its growth may be inhibited or otherwise altered. In a similar vein, a propensity towards a mental health disorder that is carried in one's genes can either develop into a full-blown illness or remain dormant, depending on the experiences that one has in their lifetime.

In order to proceed with this examination, let's have a look at the sphere of intellect and cognitive capacities. A number of investigations have led researchers to the conclusion that intelligence has a genetic component. However, genes are not authoritarian scripts; rather, they serve just as recommendations. Once again, the environment plays a significant role in determining the results. In a setting where there is no opportunity for intellectual stimulation, even if a child has genes that are linked to high intelligence, the child may never develop to their full potential.

However, as a result of the appearance of such information, numerous ethical conundrums have arisen. First and foremost among these is the utilization of genetic testing. Should people put themselves through exams to determine their mental strengths and weaknesses? And if they do, what possible applications may such information have in society? For the purpose of insurance? Do you have a job? It is imperative that extreme caution be exercised in this situation. It would be an extremely dangerous error to assign preconceived roles or to create biases based on the genetic predispositions of individuals. It is essential for humanity to keep in mind that genes denote possibilities and not certainties.

In addition, conversations on genes and mental weaknesses have the potential to unintentionally promote genetic determinism. Some people who hold this belief would conclude that they are nothing more than the sum total of their genes, which would make it pointless for them to try to overcome obstacles. This viewpoint would not only be restricting, but it would also be grossly inaccurate. Genes can make a person more susceptible to a disease, but they don't always determine it.

The field of genetic engineering is yet another significant worry in this day and age. There are many unanswered questions in this day and age, despite the fact that there is hope offered by gene-editing technologies such as CRISPR. Should human beings eliminate genes known to be connected with mental weaknesses? Such actions, notwithstanding the possibility that they will be useful, might have unintended repercussions. Diversity, which comprises a wide variety of cognitive capacities and susceptibilities, is essential to the maintenance and growth of humanity. Any attempts to create a more uniform human race would strip society of the diversity that contributes to its richness and resiliency.

Having said that, gaining an understanding of the genetic roots of mental vulnerability affords an opportunity for preventative measures that is without peer. The landscape of therapy for mental health could be dramatically altered by the introduction of early treatments, tailored therapies, and personalized drugs. This preventative strategy has the potential to lessen the impact of these vulnerabilities, so enabling individuals to lead lives that are richer and more fruitful.

Environment's Deep Impact on Mental Health

The environment in which persons live has a significant impact on the mental health of those individuals. Even the colors we look at and the noises we hear in our environment can have significant effects on the way our minds work and the way our emotions are balanced. In point of fact, one's environment continues to have a significant role in one's mental health, and the complex nature of this interaction calls for careful investigation.

To begin, let's take the surrounding natural environment into consideration. The restorative benefits that can be derived through exposure to verdant landscapes and the soothing sound of water lapping on coastlines have been recognized for a very long time. Spending time in natural settings is associated with a reduction in negative emotions such as stress, anxiety, and depression in many people. E.O. Wilson coined the term "biophilia" to describe this phenomena, which postulates that humans have a natural propensity to affiliate themselves with natural systems and species. Simply looking at images or photographs of nature, whether they are genuine or imagined, has been shown to reduce both blood pressure and heart rate in numerous studies.

On the other hand, urban environments offer a striking contrast to their rural counterparts. The constant clamor of traffic and the seemingly endless sea of concrete can, at times, make one feel completely overpowered. These kinds of environments can contribute to a phenomenon that psychologists refer to as "cognitive fatigue," which occurs when an individual's attentional resources get drained. This weariness can lead to irritation, a reduction in effectiveness in duties, and a heightened susceptibility to negative emotions. These problems are made much worse by the fact that there are not very many parks and other green spaces in urban areas. One's mental health can suffer significantly if they do not have access to appropriate environments like these.

Even the sounds in the environment can have a perceptible impact on one's state of wellbeing. The rustling of leaves, the chirping of birds, or simply the low rumble of the wind in the trees may all be quite peaceful. These auditory features stimulate the brain in a different way, making it possible for restorative processes that fight the exhaustion that is frequently encountered in metropolitan contexts. On the other hand, being subjected to jarring noises on a continuous basis might make feelings of tension and anxiety worse.

Light is one of the most important factors in determining one's mood. One's mental state can be profoundly impacted, either positively or negatively, by the presence or absence of natural light, as well as the quality of that light. Exposure to strong, natural light has been connected with better mood and vitality, but being in situations with low levels of illumination can lead to emotions of depression and despondency. This type of light, particularly during the early morning hours, helps to regulate circadian rhythms, which are crucial for the quality of sleep as well as overall cognitive function.

In the course of this discussion, colors cannot be overlooked either. They carry with them significant psychological repercussions. For example, shades of blue are known to generate feelings of calm and tranquillity, whereas hues of red are known to incite thoughts of anger and, at times, a sense of urgency. We can cultivate the mental and emotional states we want in ourselves and others by giving careful consideration to the color schemes we use in our private and public areas.

The mental health of individuals is also significantly influenced by the social situations they are exposed to. It is common knowledge that individuals experience greater happiness and fewer feelings of isolation when they are a part of tightly connected communities in which they feel a sense of belonging and purpose. On the other hand, being exposed to surroundings that are marked by antagonism, mistrust, or alienation may be detrimental to one's mental health. Therefore, encouraging healthy social relationships is, and will continue to be, a necessary step in the process of achieving comprehensive well-being.

Moreover, the significance of the architecture and spatial design of our surrounds cannot be overstated. A feeling of well-being can be achieved in environments where comfort, functionality, and aesthetics are given equal weight. On the other hand, places that are awkwardly laid out and designed might make people feel claustrophobic and uncomfortable. A setting that allows for movement, provides opportunities for rest, and presents visual interest is invariably conducive to mental well-being since it fulfills all three of these criteria.